Caring for My Pet

Cat

Susan Ring

and Katie Gillespie

MEDIA ENHANCED BOOKS

AV2 BY WEIGL™

ADDED VALUE • AUDIO VISUAL

www.av2books.com

AV² provides enriched content that supplements and complements this book. Weigl's AV² books strive to create inspired learning and engage young minds in a total learning experience.

Your AV² Media Enhanced books come alive with...

Audio
Listen to sections of the book read aloud.

Key Words
Study vocabulary, and complete a matching word activity.

Video
Watch informative video clips.

Quizzes
Test your knowledge.

Embedded Weblinks
Gain additional information for research.

Slide Show
View images and captions, and prepare a presentation.

Try This!
Complete activities and hands-on experiments.

... and much, much more!

Go to **www.av2books.com**, and enter this book's unique code.

BOOK CODE

B755180

AV² **by Weigl** brings you media enhanced books that support active learning.

Published by AV² by Weigl
350 5th Avenue, 59th Floor
New York, NY 10118
Website: www.av2books.com   www.weigl.com

Library of Congress Control Number: 2013953068
ISBN 978-1-4896-0604-4 (hardcover)
ISBN 978-1-4896-0605-1 (softcover)
ISBN 978-1-4896-0606-8 (single user eBook)
ISBN 978-1-4896-0607-5 (multi-user eBook)

Printed in the United States of America in North Mankato, Minnesota
1 2 3 4 5 6 7 8 9 0 18 17 16 15 14

012014
WEP301113

Project Coordinator: Katie Gillespie
Design and Layout: Mandy Christiansen

Every reasonable effort has been made to trace ownership and to obtain permission to reprint copyright material. The publishers would be pleased to have any errors or omissions brought to their attention so that they may be corrected in subsequent printings.

Weigl acknowledges Getty Images as its primary image supplier for this title.

Cat

Contents

Cat Care

For thousands of years, people have been drawn to cats. They are warm and loving animals. Cats have been loved, worshiped, and even feared by people. These furry creatures are both beautiful and mysterious.

Cats are not just cute and cuddly animals. They are also a big responsibility. It takes a lot of commitment to properly care for a cat. Cat owners must know what their pets need to stay healthy and happy.

It is important to give your cat the right foods, fresh water, and a safe, warm place to sleep. Cats also need to be **groomed**, given plenty of exercise, and taken for regular visits to the **veterinarian**.

91 % of owned cats in the U.S. are **spayed or neutered**.

Getting a cat fixed extends its life span by **two to five years.**

Bella, Max, and Chloe are the **three most popular** cat names in the U.S.

24% of cat owners have **three or more** cats.

There are more than **600 million** domestic cats on Earth.

🐾 Cats are one of the most popular pets. There are 95.6 million cats owned in the United States alone.

From Wild to Mild

Cats have been around for millions of years. This has been proven by the discovery of ancient **fossils**. These fossils belong to a creature called *Miacis*. This weasel-like animal lived about 50 million years ago.

🐾 Domestic cats are related to lions, tigers, and leopards.

Scientists think that cats and humans have lived together for as long as 5,000 years. In ancient Egypt, cats and people had such a close relationship that they were buried together when they died.

The most likely relatives of modern house cats are African wildcats. They were domesticated by the ancient Egyptians in 2,500 BC. These wildcats were very useful to the Egyptians because they ate mice. This helped protect people's crops from the pesky rodents, who enjoyed eating grain.

The Egyptians enjoyed having the wildcats around. They fed and cared for the friendliest cats. Over time, the wildcats became like pets to the Egyptians.

The three subfamilies of cats include *pantherinae, felinae,* **and** *acinonychinae.*

In one ancient Egyptian city, more than 300,000 cat mummies were found.

Cats have been associated with humans for at least **10,000 years.**

 House cats have flexible bodies and sharp teeth. These features help them to hunt mice, like their wildcat relatives.

Pet Profile

There are many different **breeds** of cats. They come in a variety of colors, shapes, and sizes. Most house cats are **mixed-breed** cats. Other cats are purebred. This means that the same features have been passed on from generation to generation.

Each breed of cat has distinct traits that make it special. Manx cats do not have a tail. Turkish Van cats have waterproof fur.

Domestic Cats

- Include all **nonpedigreed** cats
- Are one of the most common house cats
- Can be long-haired or short-haired
- Come in several sizes and shapes
- Have a variety of colors and markings
- Can have many different temperaments

Sphynxes

- Have wrinkly skin
- Do not have any whiskers or hair
- Enjoy being watched
- Do not like to be the only pet in the household
- Originated in 1966
- The first Sphynx came from furry parents

Persians

- Are a very loving breed
- Have long and fluffy fur
- Need plenty of daily combing, brushing, and grooming
- Come in many colors
- Have a stocky body
- Are generally quiet
- Have a flat face

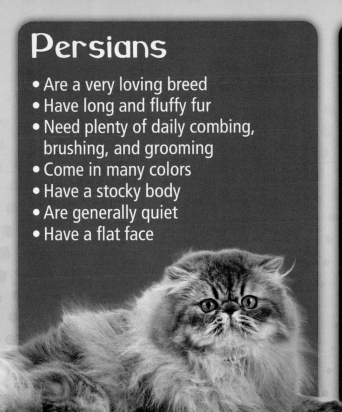

Scottish Folds

- Are easily adaptable to changes in their environment
- Are born with straight ears
- At three weeks of age, their ears fold forward
- Can be many different colors
- Have a sweet and loving temperament
- Are a very common breed
- Can have long or short hair

Siamese

- Are an intelligent breed of cat
- Have a tan body with a dark tail, ears, paws, and head
- Can be very independent
- Have large and pointed ears
- Are quite vocal and meow loudly
- Have a strong, self-assured personality
- Have short hair
- Need plenty of attention
- Have a thin and pointed head

Ragdolls

- Have light-colored body fur
- Have darker fur around their legs, tail, face, and ears
- Are friendly with children
- Have a very laid-back personality
- Enjoy grooming
- Have a long and silky coat
- Need to be brushed and combed often
- Are extremely loving cats
- Have a fluffy, large body

Picking Your Pet

Before choosing your pet cat, there are many important factors to consider. Research different breeds to find one that will be the best fit for your family. Think about these questions before choosing your furry friend.

How Much Will a Cat Cost?

The price of your pet cat will vary depending on where you go. Many cities have animal shelters, where pets have been rescued

🐾 About 26 percent of the cats owned in the United States were adopted from an animal shelter.

from the streets. Shelter cats are just waiting for a good home. Pet stores are another option. They sell several different kinds of kittens. Cats bought at a pet store will cost more than cats from a shelter. However, they often come with basic supplies. These cats will also be **vaccinated** already. The most expensive cats are purebreds. Make sure to consider other costs such as food, bedding, litter, and toys for your pet cat.

How Much Time Will My Cat Need?

Kittens can be very frisky and active. They need plenty of attention. Adult cats may require less time to care for than a kitten. Keep in mind your pet's grooming needs as well. A long-haired cat must be brushed and groomed every day. Short-haired cats can be groomed less often. All cats need their litter boxes cleaned every day.

How Will a Cat Affect My Family?

You must be careful when bringing home a new cat. It is important to make sure that no one in your family has allergies. Exposing an allergic parent or sibling to a pet can be very dangerous.

There are about **75 distinct breeds** of house cats.

Persians have been the most popular cat breed since 1871.

Domestic cats have a life span of about **13 to 20 years.**

Wildcats live for **six to eight years,** on average.

A 20-year-old house cat is about equal to a **96-year-old** human.

🐾 It is important to consider how your new cat will affect other pets in your home, such as the family dog.

Life Cycle

Your cat's needs will change as she gets older. It is fun to play with a small, cute kitten. It is just as important to make time for an adult cat. Your pet will depend on you throughout her lifetime.

Newborn Kitten

Kittens are born completely helpless. Their eyes are closed and will not open for 8 to 12 days. They cannot walk very well. Instead, kittens crawl. Most of their time is spent sleeping and drinking their mothers' milk. Always wash your hands before handling a newborn kitten. Germs on your hands can make a newborn kitten sick.

Four Weeks

At four weeks old, kittens are alert and walking. They are very curious and will explore to discover new things. They still spend much of their day sleeping. Four-week-old kittens are more independent, but will watch their mother to learn how to groom and use the litter box. They love to chase balls, strings, or ribbons.

More than Ten Years

As they get older, cats begin to need more sleep. They are less active. Their hearing and eyesight may begin to fail. Senior cats may still be playful. They may require a special diet, as some foods are hard to digest. Extra nutrients may also be needed.

One Year

One-year-old cats are considered fully grown. They spend more time on their own. Although they are independent, they still rely on you to keep them happy and healthy. At age one, cats require help to keep fit. Pet owners should have toys around the house to help their cats stay energetic.

Cat Supplies

There are some basic supplies you will need before you bring home your new pet. These include a litter box, a comfortable bed, and dishes for food and water.

Your cat should have toys to help stay active and alert. A scratching post can also be useful. This will protect your furniture, but still allow your cat to sharpen his claws. Very young kittens may need a hot-water bottle or a ticking clock in their bed. These can help them to feel less lonely.

Cleanliness is very important to cats. You must have a good brush or a comb to keep your pet cat's fur groomed. The kind of brush may depend on the length and type of your cat's hair.

A pet carrier helps keep your pet safe when traveling. It may also double as a bed for your cat.

Zzz...

Cats sleep for about **16 hours** every day.

Cats take **20 to 40 breaths** every minute.

A cat can **jump seven times** his own height.

Adult cats are in deep **sleep for 15%** of their lives.

A cat can run up to **30 miles per hour**. (50 kilometers per hour)

Cats have **32 muscles** in each ear.

Both indoor and outdoor cats require a litter box. It should never be kept near the cat's bed, food dish, or water dish. The litter box can be covered or open. Some cats may be trained to use a toilet. They do not need a litter box at all.

A cat's bed can be bought from a pet supply store. It should be warm and placed away from drafts. Some cats are just as happy sleeping in a blanket-lined cardboard box as in a bed. Do not be surprised if your cat chooses his own sleeping arrangements. Many cats enjoy having a special spot that is their own.

Feeding a Feline

Cats can be quite fussy when it comes to meals. This is why you must change your cat's food from time to time. If you do not vary what your cat eats, she may become so used to one food that she refuses to eat anything else.

What Should I Feed My Cat?

Cat food comes in different formulas. Canned, wet food is available in a variety of flavors. It can give your cat all of the vitamins she needs to stay healthy.

You should also feed your cat dry food. It helps to clean and strengthen your cat's teeth. Most pet owners give their cats a balance of half wet and half dry food. On occasion, you may also want to feed your cat fresh food. Cats love to eat turkey or chicken.

🐾 Cats should be fed twice a day. A typical meal for a cat is equal to about five mice.

When feeding your cat fresh fish, it is important to remove all of the bones. You must also make sure to keep your cat's water dish full. Change the water often to keep it fresh and clean.

What Do Cats Like?

Most cats love treats. These come in many different sizes, shapes, and flavors. Make sure you only give your cat treats once in awhile. They do not offer as much nutrition as your cat's food. It is also important for cats to have some fat in their diet. Their bodies are unable to produce it on their own.

The average house cat weighs **8 to 11 pounds.** (4 to 5 kilograms)

The **heaviest** domestic cat weighed more than **46 pounds**. (21 kg)

Tap water should sit for **24 hours** before a cat drinks it.

A cat's sense of smell is **14 times better** than a human's.

In the U.S., **more money** is spent on cat food than baby food **each year.**

$ $ $ $ $ $

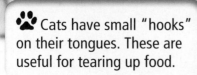
Cats have small "hooks" on their tongues. These are useful for tearing up food.

Fast and Furry

From domestic cats to wildcats, all cats have certain features in common. The majority of cats have fur on their bodies. This helps to keep them warm.

Cats are quick, strong, **agile**, and intelligent. They have keen senses, which are very sensitive. These traits make cats exceptionally good hunters.

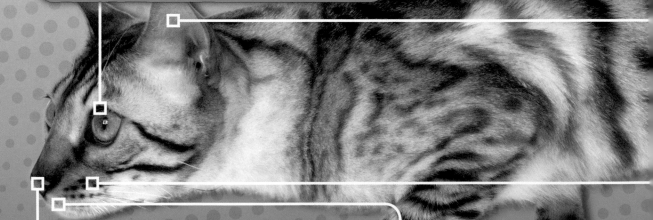

Eyes

In low light, a cat's pupils grow very round and large. This lets more light enter. In bright light, a cat's pupils narrow to slits.

Nose

Cats have a very sharp sense of smell. Kittens use it to guide them before they are able to see.

Mouth

Cats have rough tongues for drinking and grooming. They use their sharp, pointed teeth to rip meat.

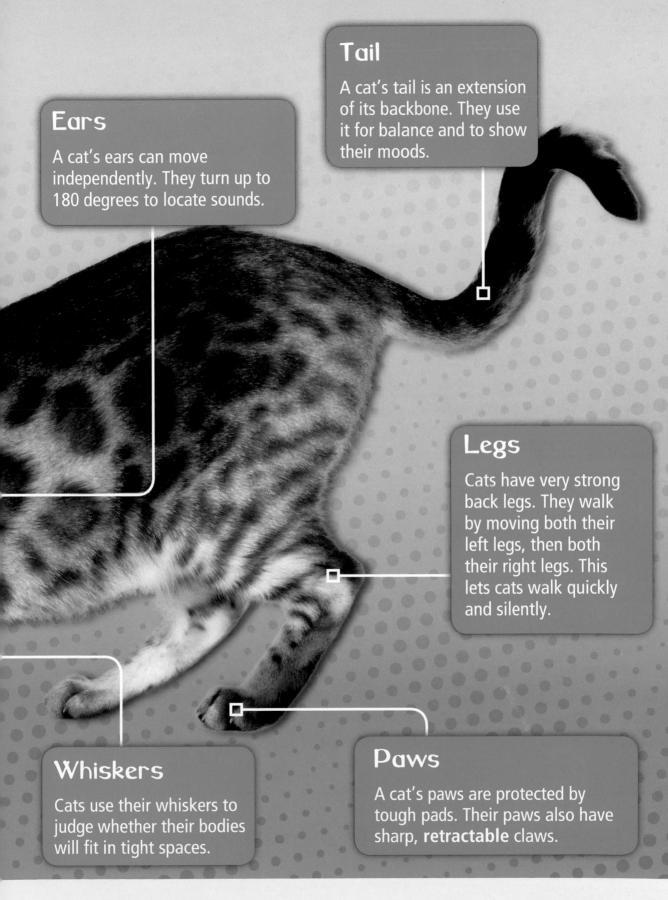

Tail

A cat's tail is an extension of its backbone. They use it for balance and to show their moods.

Ears

A cat's ears can move independently. They turn up to 180 degrees to locate sounds.

Legs

Cats have very strong back legs. They walk by moving both their left legs, then both their right legs. This lets cats walk quickly and silently.

Whiskers

Cats use their whiskers to judge whether their bodies will fit in tight spaces.

Paws

A cat's paws are protected by tough pads. Their paws also have sharp, **retractable** claws.

Purr-fect Grooming

It is normal for your cat to spend a lot of time grooming himself. Cats use their rough tongues like combs to remove dirt and twigs from their fur. They also lick their paws and use them to clean their faces, like a washcloth.

Cats need to be groomed by their owners as well. Regular grooming can help a kitten adapt to being handled. It also allows you to check your cat's skin and fur for burrs or **mats**.

It is important to brush your cat often, especially if he has long hair. This will prevent knots and tangles. To groom your cat, hold him on your lap or in front of you on the floor.

Cats have **five toes** on their front paws.

A cat's night vision is **six times better** than a human's.

Adult cats have **30 teeth.**

Cats have **four toes** on their back paws.

Cats must have their teeth cleaned at least **once a year.**

Most cats do not need to be bathed. Instead, they lick their coats to keep them clean.

Slowly check your cat's whole body for anything out of the ordinary. Then, brush downward gently. You should move from the head to the tail. After brushing, you should use a comb to finish grooming a long-haired cat.

Your cat may purr when he is being brushed. Regular grooming helps prevent hairballs. If a cat swallows too much fur while grooming himself, this fur can block the stomach. Keeping your cat groomed will make sure he is healthy. It will also create a bond between you and your cat.

Healthy and Happy

A healthy cat is a happy cat. Loving and caring for your cat will help keep her happy. You should also make sure your cat is well-groomed, given the right foods, and getting regular exercise. Take your pet to a veterinarian that makes you and your cat feel comfortable.

Your veterinarian will be able to answer any questions you may have about your cat's health or behavior. He will also give your cat regular vaccinations. These will protect your cat from common illnesses.

Different types of cats have special concerns. Light-colored cats are easily sunburned. It is best for them to stay out of the sunlight, when possible.

You will get to know your cat's personality over time. As you do, you will learn her habits and patterns. This will help you to notice if something is wrong. Pay attention to your cat's schedule. Is she eating more or less than normal? Is she drinking more water than usual? If so, this could mean that your cat is sick.

Sneezing or coughing are other symptoms that may mean your cat is sick. Be aware of any wound licking or limping. These might indicate that your cat needs veterinary care. It is important for you to make sure that your home is safe for your cat.

Some human foods and medicines can be poisonous to pets. Never give a cat chocolate or aspirin.

Kittens should get their first vaccinations when they are about **nine weeks** old.

Cats should visit the vet **once or twice a year.**

A cat's normal pulse rate is **130 to 240** beats per minute.

A cat's average temperature is **100 to 103° Fahrenheit**. (38 to 39° Celsius)

You will only see a cat's **third eyelid** when she is not feeling well.

Cat Behavior

Although cats are often independent, they do like to play and bond with their owner. Indoor cats require plenty of toys and activities. Outdoor cats need attention too. It is important for you to love and spend time with your cat.

Cats are very intelligent. They can be trained and disciplined. If your cat behaves badly, correct him with a firm "no." Never hit your cat if he is naughty. When your cat does something good, reward him with a hug or a treat.

🐾 Kittens love to chase toys and play fight. Playing helps them learn and practice new skills for hunting.

Your cat will communicate with you in many ways. Even though he cannot speak, he can let you know how he is feeling. Your cat may move his tail to show that he is upset or excited. When he is grooming, your cat probably wants to be left alone. When he rubs his head against you, he wants attention.

Cats have special scent glands between their eye and ear. Rubbing them against objects or people will mark them. Your cat will feel more comfortable when he recognizes his own scent on you.

Pet Peeves

Cats do not like:

- closed doors
- having their tails pulled
- being poked
- loud noises or barking dogs
- not enough attention
- too much attention
- being moved while sleeping

Cats make different sounds when they are scared, angry, or happy. Over time, you will learn to understand how your cat feels when he hisses or purrs.

Cats kill **6.9 to 20.7 billion** small mammals every year.

Cats make more than **100** different **vocal sounds**.

meow meow meow

If left uncontrolled, cats may have **three to seven** kittens every **four months.**

Alice's Adventures in Wonderland by Lewis Carroll features the Cheshire Cat, one of the most famous felines in literary history.

Cat Tales

From authors to inventors, many important people have been friends to felines. Mark Twain, who wrote *The Adventures of Huckleberry Finn*; Daniel Boone, the legendary American frontiersman; and Sir Isaac Newton, who discovered the theory of gravity and invented the first cat-flap door, are all well-known for their fondness for cats.

Several U.S. presidents have also been identified as cat lovers, including George Washington and Abraham Lincoln. President Theodore Roosevelt owned a gray cat named Slippers, who had six toes on each foot. Slippers was allowed to attend large state dinners at the White House and sit wherever he wanted. Before he became president, Governor Ronald Reagan signed a bill that made it illegal to kick cats.

Cats have also been featured in a variety of television shows, movies, books, fables, and stories. Sylvester the Cat is famous for appearing with Tweety Bird in more than 40 cartoons. In 1947, the pair starred in a short film called *Tweety Pie*, which earned Warner Brothers its first Academy Award.

Of Cats and Men

People often develop meaningful relationships with their pets. Approximately 95 percent of cat owners admit that they talk to their furry friends on a regular basis. Cats can be an important part of their owners' lives. They are typically thought of as members of the family.

In 1950, a four-month-old kitten in Switzerland followed mountain climbers all the way to the top of the 14,691-foot (4,478-meter) Matterhorn in the Swiss Alps.

Abraham Lincoln was the **first U.S. president** to bring a cat into the White House.

About **90%** of cats survive after falling from a high-rise building.

In **1987**, cats overtook dogs as the **most popular** pet in the U.S.

Pet Puzzlers

What do you know about cats? If you can answer the following questions correctly, you may be ready to own a cat.

1. What does a cat use her whiskers for?

To judge whether their bodies will fit in tight spaces

2. What should you feed your cat?

A combination of wet food, dry food, fresh food, and treats

3. When should your cat be vaccinated?

Around nine weeks of age

4. What kinds of cats are easily sunburned?

Light-colored cats

5. Why is regular grooming so important?

Regular grooming helps to keep your cat healthy. It prevents hairballs from forming and allows you to form a bond with your cat.

6. How do cats communicate with their owners?

By moving their tails, making purring or hissing noises, and rubbing their heads on their owners

7. What are some supplies you need for your pet cat?

A warm bed, toys, food and water dishes, a brush and comb, and a litter box

8. Why must you wash your hands when handling a newborn kitten?

Newborn kittens are very sensitive, and germs on your hands might make them sick.

9. How should you reward your cat?

With a hug or a treat

10. How long have cats been domesticated?

5,000 years

Calling Your Cat

Before you bring home your pet cat, brainstorm some cat names you like. Some names may work better for a female cat. Others may suit a male cat. Here are just a few suggestions.

Garfield

Ginger

Sylvester

Kitty

Fluffy

Smokey

Socks

Sam

Snuggles

Key Words

agile: athletic; moves easily

breeds: groups of animals that share specific characteristics

fossils: remains of animals and plants from long ago, found in rocks

groomed: cleaned by removing dirt from fur

mats: tangles, knots, and clumps of fur

mixed-breed: a cat whose parents and relatives are a mixture of different cat breeds

nonpedigreed: not having a pure line of ancestors

retractable: able to withdraw

vaccinated: injected with medicines that help prevent certain diseases or illnesses

veterinarian: animal doctor

Index

Log on to www.av2books.com

AV² by Weigl brings you media enhanced books that support active learning. Go to www.av2books.com, and enter the special code found on page 2 of this book. You will gain access to enriched and enhanced content that supplements and complements this book. Content includes video, audio, weblinks, quizzes, a slide show, and activities.

AV² Online Navigation

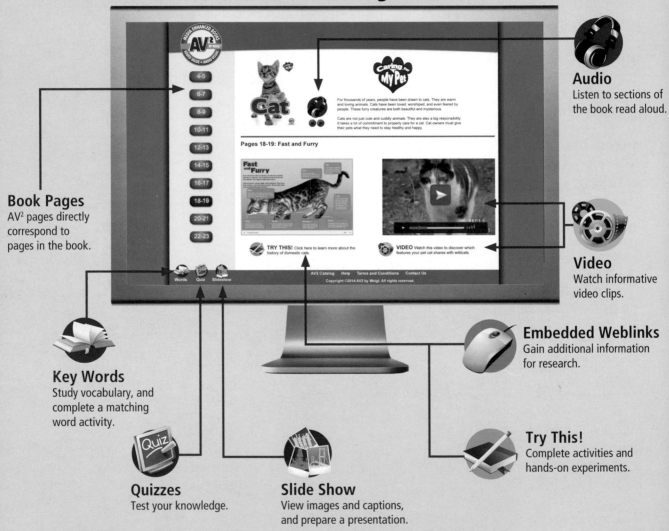

Audio
Listen to sections of the book read aloud.

Book Pages
AV² pages directly correspond to pages in the book.

Video
Watch informative video clips.

Key Words
Study vocabulary, and complete a matching word activity.

Embedded Weblinks
Gain additional information for research.

Quizzes
Test your knowledge.

Slide Show
View images and captions, and prepare a presentation.

Try This!
Complete activities and hands-on experiments.

AV² was built to bridge the gap between print and digital. We encourage you to tell us what you like and what you want to see in the future.

Sign up to be an AV² Ambassador at www.av2books.com/ambassador.